GEO DETECTIVES
VOLCANOES & EARTHQUAKES

Anita Ganeri & Chris Oxlade

Illustrated by **Pau Morgan**

Curriculum consultant **Richard Hatwood**

Quarto is the authority on a wide range of topics.

Quarto educates, entertains and enriches the lives of our readers—enthusiasts and lovers of hands-on living.

www.quartoknows.com

Author: Anita Ganeri and Chris Oxlade
Illustrator: Pau Morgan
Consultant: Michael Bright
Curriculum consultant: Richard Hatwood
Editor: Harriet Stone
Designer: Sarah Chapman-Suire
Editorial Director: Laura Knowles

© 2019 Quarto Publishing plc
This edition first published in 2019
by QEB Publishing,
an imprint of The Quarto Group.
6 Orchard Road, Suite 100
Lake Forest, CA 92630
T: +1 949 380 7510
F: +1 949 380 7575
www.QuartoKnows.com

A CIP record for this book is available from the Library of Congress.

ISBN 978 0 7112 4461 0

Manufactured in Guangdong, China TT072019

9 8 7 6 5 4 3 2 1

Picture Credits
(t=top, b=bottom, l=left, r=right, fc=front cover)

Shutterstock
fc Benjamin Albiach Galan, 7 Rost9, 9tr shihina,
9mr Jurek Adamski, 9br Pierre Leclerc, 10bl Ralf Lehmann,
10mr Benjamin Albiach Galan, 12 J. Helgason,
13br The Wild Eyed, 21 Steve Collender,
23r tishomir, 25 Smallcreative, 26 Noska Photo

Getty
10t TIBTA PANGIN/AFP/Getty Images

Alamy
13t RGB Ventures / SuperStock, 17 robertharding,
14-15b incamerastock, 19l Panther Media GmbH,
20tl icollection

Wikimediacommons
23l U.S. Army

Contents

Be a Geo Detective   4
Cracked Earth   6
Inside a Volcano   8
Eruption!   10
Famous Volcanoes   12
Volcano Science   14
Earthquake Faults   16
Spreading Waves   18
Earthquake Damage   20

Famous Earthquakes   22
Tsunamis   24
Earthquake Safety and Rescue 26

Geo Detective quiz   28
Glossary   29
Authors' note   30
Find out more   30
Notes for teachers & parents 31
Index   32

Be a Geo Detective

Let's join Ava and George on a journey exploring the world of volcanoes and earthquakes. They'll be using their detective skills to find out what causes volcanoes to explode and earthquakes to shake the ground. You can help by trying out the activities for yourself.

The Geo Detectives are ready to go!

A volcano is a place where **molten** rock called **magma** comes out from deep under the ground. When the molten rock reaches the surface we call it **lava**.

Boom! That volcano is erupting! We're going to investigate inside the Earth to find out why volcanoes erupt.

GEO FACT

There are over 1.5 million earthquakes every year! That's about 4,000 a day. Luckily, most of them are too gentle for us to feel.

Whoa! The ground under my feet is cracking. The buildings are wobbling, and so am I! Let's find out why this happens.

An earthquake makes the ground shake from side to side and up and down.

Cracked Earth

What would you find if you dug deep down into the Earth? The answer is lots of rock! Join the Geo Detectives to explore below the surface of our planet.

The Earth is made up of thick layers of rock. We live on the outside layer, which is called the **crust**. Earth's crust is covered in oceans, soil, and plants, as well as people and animals! It's broken into huge pieces called **tectonic plates**.

The middle part of the Earth is called the **core**. The core is hard in the middle and soft on the outside. Around the core is a thick layer of rock called the **mantle**. The rock in the mantle is hot and soft. It moves around very slowly, which makes the tectonic plates on the crust move too.

> Phew! It's red-hot down here. This must be the Earth's core.

GEO FACT

The temperature at Earth's core is a roasting 10,830 degrees Fahrenheit (6,000 degrees Celsius). That's 30 times hotter than an oven!

CORE

Cookie Plates

See what happens to the tectonic plates on the Earth's crust, using a soggy cookie!

What you need:
- crumbly cookie
- plate
- cup of water

1. Break a cookie in half.

2. Dip each half into a cup of water for about two seconds.

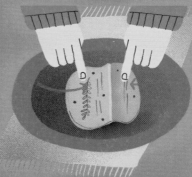

3. Put the pieces on a plate and push the damp sides into each other.

The edges of the cookie crumple into a heap. This is what happens when two tectonic plates move toward each other. The rocky plates get bent and broken, which makes an earthquake.

The Earth's crust is thin and hard, like the crust on a loaf of bread!

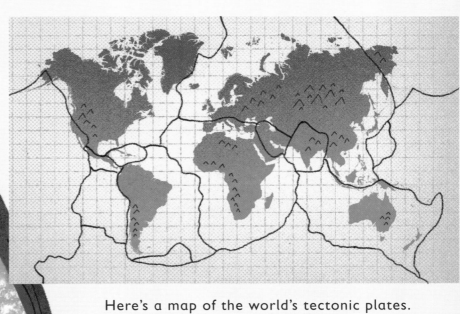

Here's a map of the world's tectonic plates. Can you see the lines where the plates meet each other? Most volcanoes and earthquakes happen near these lines.

MANTLE

—— CRUST

Inside a Volcano

All volcanoes are made of layers of rock, but not all volcanoes are the same shape. Ava and George are learning about different types of volcano. Let's take a closer look!

Every volcano has a pipe called a **vent** and a **crater** at the top. Deep under the volcano there is a big space called the **magma chamber**. It's full of molten rock called magma.

Look what's happening inside this volcano. Magma from the magma chamber is rising up the vent and spurting out of the crater. The volcano is erupting!

GEO FACT

The tallest volcanoes on Earth are under the sea. Only the top of an undersea volcano can be seen, sticking out as an island above the waves.

There are three main types of volcano. George is looking at a volcano with tall, steep sides. It must be a composite cone!

A **composite cone** volcano has tall, steep sides, made from ash and sticky molten rock.

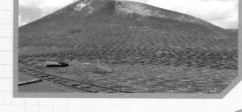

A **shield** volcano is shaped like an upside-down shield, short and wide.

What you need:
• popcorn
• large plate
• small cup
• large straw

A **cinder cone** is a small volcano made of rocky lumps called **cinders**.

Popcorn Cinder Cone

Make a popcorn volcano to see how gas blows cinders out of a crater.

1. Put the cup in the middle of the plate.

2. Put popcorn around the cup to make a wide cone.

3. Fill the cup with more popcorn.

4. Push one end of the straw into the cup and blow sharply. Watch the popcorn fly upward and land on the cone!

Can you blow all the cinders out of the cup in ten seconds?

The flying popcorn pieces are like cinders. They fly from the volcano's crater and land around it. They gradually build up to make a cone.

Eruption!

When a volcano erupts, magma blasts out of its crater and flies into the air as hot lava. The Geo Detectives are investigating what else happens during an eruption. What can you see?

Hot gas builds up underground and blows the magma upward to make spectacular glowing fountains of lava. The lava also runs downhill in red-hot rivers called **lava flows**.

The lava flow is slowing down here. It must be cooling and turning into solid rock.

Sandpit Volcano

Build a model volcano and create an eruption!

What you need:
- sand
- two plastic cups
- vinegar
- baking soda
- red food coloring

1. Outdoors, build a cone of damp sand about 8 inches (20 cm) high.

2. Push one plastic cup, facing upward, into the top of the cone and mold the sand around it.

3. Put a few teaspoons of baking soda into the cup.

4. Half fill the other cup with vinegar and add a few drops of red food coloring.

5. Pour the vinegar into the cup inside your volcano.

Some volcanoes send huge clouds of ash into the sky when they erupt. The clouds are called **eruption columns** and can be up to 6 miles (10 km) tall. That's as long as 100 football fields!

Ugh! There's a thick layer of dust on everything—including me. It's ash falling from the sky.

When you mix vinegar and baking soda together, it makes a gas.

The bubbles of gas push the mixture out, just like in a real volcano.

GEO FACT

Lava can flow at up to 37 miles (60 km) per hour. That's much faster than you could run or cycle!

Famous Volcanoes

Some volcanoes are world-famous because of their spectacular eruptions. Find out about some famous eruptions with Ava and George. Can you guess what type of volcano these are from the pictures?

Eyjafjallajökull (Iceland)
This volcano erupted in 2010. An ash cloud from the eruption spread over northern Europe.

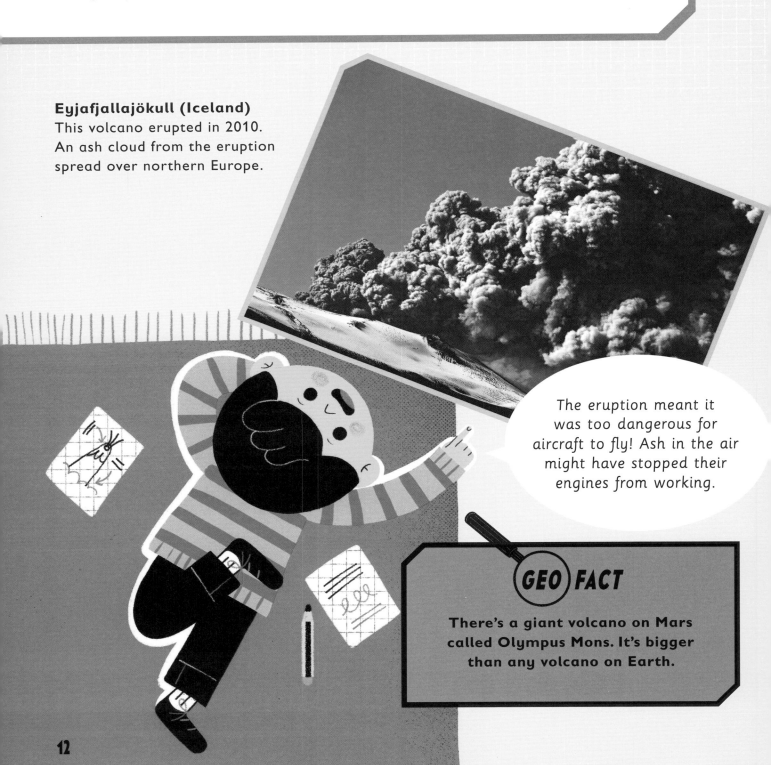

The eruption meant it was too dangerous for aircraft to fly! Ash in the air might have stopped their engines from working.

GEO FACT

There's a giant volcano on Mars called Olympus Mons. It's bigger than any volcano on Earth.

Kilauea (Hawaii)
Kilauea erupts often. Long rivers of lava flow down to the sea.

Ka-boom! The island that Krakatoa stood on almost completely disappeared. A new volcano is now growing in its place.

Krakatoa (Indonesia)
Krakatoa blew itself to pieces in 1883. People heard the explosion thousands of miles away.

What you need:
- large sheets of paper
- pens
- glue
- scissors (ask an adult for help)

Volcano Map-maker

Create a map of the world's most famous volcanoes. What do you notice about their locations?

1. Draw or print out a large map of the world.

2. Draw some volcanoes about 1 inch (about 3 cm) high on a piece of paper and cut them out.

3. Stick volcano pictures on the map in the location of Kilauea, Krakatoa, and Eyjafjallajökull.

4. Research and add some other famous volcanoes, such as Mount Fuji, Cotopaxi, Mount St. Helens, and Vesuvius. Label each volcano.

Compare your map to the map of tectonic plates on page 7. Most volcanoes happen along the lines between these plates. The circle of volcanoes around the Pacific Ocean is called the Ring of Fire.

Volcano Science

Scientists who study volcanoes are called **volcanologists**. The **Geo Detectives** are helping these volcanologists learn about this lava flow. Put on your shiny suit and join them!

This volcanologist is collecting lava. She will study the lava in a lab once it has cooled down.

Lava and ash can destroy homes and injure people who live near to volcanoes. Volcanologists climb volcanoes to set up their measuring equipment. This helps to warn people if an eruption is going to happen soon.

Collecting lava samples looks like a dangerous job! The volcanologists get really close to the hot lava flow.

These shiny suits are protecting us from the lava's heat. Phew!

Heat-resistant Materials

What you need:
- chocolate bar
- aluminum foil
- plastic wrap
- black paper
- plate

Which materials are best at protecting against heat? Complete this chocolaty experiment to find out for yourself.

1. Break off four pieces of chocolate from the bar.

2. Wrap one piece in aluminum foil, one in plastic wrap, one in black paper, and leave one unwrapped.

3. Put the pieces of chocolate on a plate and leave it somewhere sunny.

4. Every five minutes, gently press the pieces to see which ones have melted. Which piece do you think will be the last to melt?

This is a GPS movement sensor. It detects tiny movements in the ground that happen before an eruption. The ground moves when magma shifts underground.

The chocolate wrapped in black paper will be the first to melt, as the color black absorbs the most heat. The chocolate wrapped in foil will be the last to melt. Heat bounces off the shiny foil, keeping the chocolate cool. In the same way, volcanologists wear shiny suits so the lava's heat bounces off.

GEO FACT

In chilly Iceland, the heat from volcanoes helps farmers to grow bananas!

Earthquake Faults

Now that we've explored volcanoes, let's take a closer look at another dangerous natural event: earthquakes. The Geo Detectives are finding out what causes these mega movements in the Earth.

We know the Earth's crust is split into tectonic plates. The cracks between these plates are called **faults**. The plates on either side of a fault slide against each other when magma in the mantle moves around.

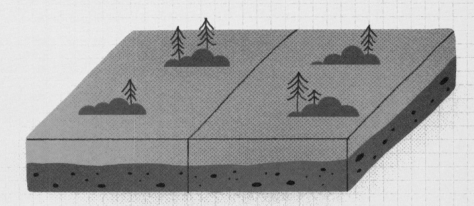

When the plates get stuck and suddenly move again, an earthquake happens. Ava is showing us the movement by pushing the plates. A slip like this causes a big earthquake.

Heave! A fault can be jammed up for hundreds of years and then slip suddenly, when the pressure gets too great.

GEO FACT

The San Andreas Fault in the USA and the Anatolian Fault in Turkey are so big they can be seen from space!

Look at that! The slip must have caused a big earthquake.

Sometimes you can see where a fault has slipped. A fault goes right across these fields.

What you need:
• bread
• jam
• knife (ask an adult for help)

Sliding Sandwiches

Use jam sandwiches to see how different faults move during an earthquake.

1. Make a jam sandwich using two slices of bread.

2. Spread more jam on top of the sandwich and add another slice of bread. The layers represent layers of rock in the Earth's crust.

3. Cut the sandwich in half to make two blocks.

4. Cut one block in half with a vertical cut and cut the other in half with a diagonal cut.

5. Use your sandwich blocks to demonstrate these three types of earthquake.

This is called a reverse fault. One plate gets pushed beneath the other.

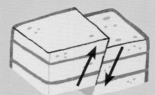

This is called a normal fault. It's made when rocks get pulled apart.

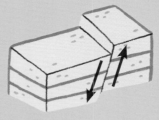

This is called a strike-slip fault. The plates scrape their edges together.

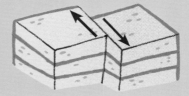

Spreading Waves

When a fault slips suddenly, the quake spreads out through the crust until it reaches the surface, where we can feel it. Join the **Geo Detectives** to learn how an earthquake travels, and how it can be measured.

Scientists who study earthquakes are called **seismologists**. They use machines called **seismographs**, which draw graphs to show how much the ground shakes during an earthquake.

The earthquake waves spread across the surface. They make the ground shake up and down and from side to side.

A seismograph picks up tiny vibrations in the ground that we can't feel with our feet.

Look at how the earthquake waves move. They travel like ripples on a pond after you throw in a pebble.

GEO FACT

The strength of an earthquake is measured using a magnitude scale. An earthquake that measures 7 or more is a powerful earthquake.

The place where a fault slips and causes an earthquake is called the **focus**. Earthquake waves spread out from the focus in every direction.

Model Seismograph

Make your very own seismograph to measure quakes.

What you need:
- cardboard box
- string
- small plastic pot
- felt-tip pen
- coins
- plain paper
- tape

1. Put the box on its side. Using a pen, pierce two holes in the top surface of the box 2 inches (5 cm) apart.

2. Pierce a hole in the bottom of the plastic pot.

3. Push the felt-tip pen out through the hole in the pot and tape it in place.

4. Put a few coins in the pot to make it heavier.

5. Stick a piece of string on each side of the pot and feed the strings through the holes in the box.

6. Adjust the strings so the tip of the pen is just touching the bottom of the box, and tape in place.

7. Place the paper in the box under the pen.

8. Put the box on a table. Shake the table and slowly pull the paper out of the box at the same time. The pen should draw a wiggly line on the paper.

As the table shakes, the box shakes too, but the pot and pen stay still. The pen records the shaking on the paper. A seismograph works in the same way, when an earthquake happens.

Earthquake Damage

When an earthquake strikes, the ground begins to wobble. It shakes gently at first but then more violently. Lights sway around, furniture falls over —and so could you! Ava and George are looking at what else happens during an earthquake.

Simple buildings such as stone huts can't survive a strong earthquake. Sometimes even concrete buildings collapse.

What you need:
- tray
- two round pencils
- wooden building blocks
- sticky putty
- straws

Earthquake Challenge

Who can make the best quake-resistant building? Take this challenge to find out.

1. Put two pencils on a table about 8 inches (20 cm) apart.

2. Put the tray on top of the pencils. Check to make sure that the tray rolls from side to side.

3. Each player makes a building with wooden blocks, sticky putty, and straws.

4. Now test your buildings! Put them all on the tray and gently roll it from side to side. This is like the ground shaking during an earthquake.

5. Shake the tray faster, until only one building is left standing. Who is the winner?

When earthquakes are weak, most buildings stay standing. The stronger an earthquake gets, the more likely it is that buildings will crash to the ground.

These skyscrapers have stayed standing up because they have strong metal frames inside.

Look at these bent railways tracks! They show that the ground has been shaken from side to side.

Earthquakes crack the ground leaving big holes. Roads break up and walls and fences are ripped apart.

GEO FACT

Sometimes the shaking makes the soil turn soft and runny. Cars and buildings sink into it!

Famous Earthquakes

Are you ready to investigate some of the most famous earthquakes in history with the Geo Detectives? They are famous because they were very powerful and did lots of damage.

San Francisco (USA)

A huge earthquake hit the city of San Francisco in 1906. Hundreds of wooden and brick buildings collapsed. Fires broke out and destroyed even more buildings.

It looks like people didn't know how to make earthquake-proof buildings back then!

GEO FACT

Experts think that another big earthquake could hit San Francisco at any time.

Sinking Soil

What you need:
- large plastic bowl
- sand
- water
- wooden block
- toy hammer

See how earthquakes cause buildings to sink into the ground with this fun experiment.

1. Fill the bowl with damp sand about 2 inches (5 cm) deep.

2. Stand a wooden block on its end on the sand.

3. Hit the sand with the toy hammer, again and again. This makes the sand shake like it would in an earthquake. What happens to the sand and the wooden block?

The shaking makes the damp sand become like a liquid. The wooden block sinks and falls over. This is what happened to buildings during the Alaskan earthquake.

Anchorage (Alaska, USA)
In 1964 an earthquake hit Alaska in North America. In the city of Anchorage, buildings collapsed because the soil went soft. The earthquake also started a **tsunami**, which reached Japan, far away across the Pacific Ocean.

Kobe (Japan)
Japan is close to the edge of a tectonic plate, so many earthquakes happen here. In 1995 the city of Kobe was badly damaged by a quake. Even some buildings that were made to resist earthquakes collapsed.

A tsunami is a giant wave!

23

Tsunamis

When you jump into a swimming pool, a wave spreads out across the water. When an earthquake happens under the sea, a giant wave spreads out in the same way. This is called a tsunami. Let's take a look at the stages of a tsunami with the Geo Detectives.

An earthquake has happened far out at sea. The waves roll across the sea toward the land.

The seabed suddenly rises or falls during the earthquake. This sets off a tsunami.

Just before a tsunami arrives, the sea moves away from the coast, as though someone has pulled the plug out of a bathtub.

A big tsunami can lift up boats and carry them inland. The boats are left behind when the water drains back into the sea.

What you need:
- two planks of wood about 3 feet (90 cm) long
- two planks of wood about 1.5 feet (45 cm) long
- sheet of wood about 6 x 8 inches (15 x 20 cm)
- large plastic sheet

Tsunami Tank

See how you can cause a big wave with your own model tsunami.

1. Outdoors, arrange the two long planks of wood and the two short planks of wood to make a rectangle.

2. Prop up the sheet of wood at one end of the rectangle to make a slope. This is your beach.

3. Cover the rectangle with the plastic sheet.

4. Pour water into the plastic sheet. The sheet will sink into the rectangle.

5. Start a tsunami wave by quickly pushing your hand into the tank at the opposite end to the slope.

Your hand is acting like the force of an earthquake. Watch the wave move along the tank and sweep up the slope. The wave gets higher as it moves up the beach.

Earthquake Safety and Rescue

It's very difficult to tell when an earthquake is going to happen, but you can be ready in case one strikes. In some places, people practice earthquake **drills**. Ava is practicing a drill so that she is ready in case the real thing happens one day.

These rescue dogs have an incredible sense of smell. They are helping to sniff out people in the rubble.

After a big earthquake, people might be trapped in collapsed buildings. Emergency teams work hard to find them.

GEO FACT

Rescuers use very sensitive microphones to listen for people who may be trapped.

Practice an Earthquake Drill

Imagine you feel the ground start to shake. Follow these simple steps to stay safe.

1. DUCK down so that you are on your knees.

2. COVER your head, or take COVER under a table or desk.

3. HOLD onto something, such as a table leg.

4. Don't stand up until the shaking stops.

An earthquake **emergency kit** includes food and drink, warm blankets, a flashlight, and a first-aid kit.

When an earthquake happens, furniture can topple over and ceilings can fall down. Ava is practicing an earthquake drill.

The desk is really strong. It will stop things from hitting me on the head.

Most earthquakes shake the ground for 10 to 30 seconds. It's not always safe after the shaking stops because more earthquakes, called **aftershocks**, can follow the main quake.

Geo Detective quiz

Now help Ava and George answer these Geo Detective questions.
How much did you learn as you explored volcanoes and earthquakes?

1. What is the rocky outside layer of Earth called?

2. What's the name of the plates on the outside layer of the Earth?

3. What shape is a composite cone volcano?

4. Where is a volcano's crater?

5. What is a river of lava called?

6. Why do volcanologists wear shiny suits?

7. What is a fault?

8. What does a seismologist do?

9. What does a seismograph measure?

10. How do dogs help rescuers after an earthquake?

11. What is the name of the fault that caused the San Francisco earthquake?

12. What happened to the soil during the 1964 Alaskan earthquake?

13. Where does a tsunami happen?

14. What should you do if you feel an earthquake starting?

Glossary

aftershock earthquake that happens a few minutes or hours after a larger earthquake

cinder cone volcano small volcano made from cinders that often forms on the slopes of a larger volcano

cinders small chunks of rock made when bits of lava are thrown into the air and become solid before they land

composite cone volcano type of volcano that has steep sides and is made up of layers of ash and lava

core very middle part of the Earth

crater hole in the top of a volcano where lava comes out

crust the hard, rocky outer layer of the Earth

drill training for an event by practicing following instructions

emergency kit things that might be needed after an earthquake, such as water, food, a flashlight, and blankets

eruption column tall cloud of hot gas and ash above an erupting volcano

fault huge crack in the Earth's crust that can slip, causing an earthquake

focus place inside the Earth's crust where an earthquake starts

lava molten rock that bursts from a volcano and flows across the ground

lava flow river of lava that flows from a volcano

magma molten rock under the Earth's crust

magma chamber space under a volcano which fills with magma before a volcano erupts

mantle thickest layer of the Earth, between the core and the crust, made from soft, hot rock

molten hot enough to be melted

seismograph device that detects movement and shaking caused by earthquakes

seismologist scientist who studies earthquakes

shield volcano wide volcano made from cooled lava

tectonic plate one of the giant plates that the Earth's crust is cracked into

tsunami powerful ocean wave that can flood a coast, set off by an earthquake that happens under the sea

vent hole where gas and steam comes out of a volcano

volcanologist scientist who studies volcanoes

Authors' note

Hello,
We hope you have enjoyed reading with the Geo Detectives! Did you learn lots about volcanoes and earthquakes? Did you try out all the experiments?

We have written many books about lots of different topics, from monster trucks to the solar system, but the Earth we live on is always one of our favorite topics. We both enjoy being outdoors and two of our favorite hobbies are rock climbing and hill walking. Do you enjoy being outside? Our hobbies have given us an interest in rocks and how mountains and other features of the landscape are built up and worn away.

We've visited a few volcanoes on our travels, including Etna and Stromboli, in Italy, and several volcanoes in Iceland. They are amazing places and seeing steam, ash, and lava spew from the Earth makes you realize that the planet is alive beneath our feet. While in Iceland we experienced an earthquake, too. It was only a small quake but still a bit scary. We're quite pleased that we live in England, where there are no volcanoes, and only tiny earthquakes to worry about!

Chris Oxlade & Anita Ganeri

Find out more

Visit these websites to find out more about volcanoes and earthquakes.

earthquake.usgs.gov/learn/kids/
Read cool facts, projects, and the latest information about earthquakes around the world on this United States Geological Survey website.

www.ready.gov/kids/know-the-facts
Learn how to be earthquake and volcano ready, on this website from the United States Department of Homeland Security.

www.bbc.com/bitesize/articles/zd9cxyc
Discover more about volcanoes with BBC Bitesize.

www.bbc.com/bitesize/articles/zj89t39
Discover more about earthquakes with BBC Bitesize.

Notes for teachers & parents

Take the learning further with these extra activities and discussion points for in the classroom, or at home.

Many people live in places that have volcanic eruptions and earthquakes. Ask the children how they would feel living in a place that had eruptions and earthquakes. Why might people choose to live there and not move away?

In 2010, the Eyjafjallajökull volcano in Iceland erupted. This caused lots of disruption to air travel. Airplanes couldn't fly across most of Europe for over 6 days. Can the children find out what happened and why?

Some people have turned the dangers of living beside a volcano into positives. Can the children find out any good things about living near a volcano?

People have developed some clever ways of living in places that have earthquakes. Research how people in Japan protect themselves from earthquakes.

What can the children find out about the Pacific Ring of Fire? Why do they think it is called this?

Montserrat is a Caribbean island that has experienced a number of volcanic eruptions. Locate Montserrat on a map with the children. What happened in Montserrat after the volcano last erupted? How did people's lives change after the eruption?

Tsunamis are hard to predict and can cause lots of damage. How can people in coastal areas predict when a tsunami may happen? Can the children remember any information from this book that might help them?

The plates at the San Andreas Fault line in San Francisco are moving alongside each other. Why do we not find volcanoes here?

Is Iceland growing in size? Can the children find out the answer to this question and the reason why?

Index

aftershocks 27, 29
Anatolian Fault
    (Turkey) 16
Anchorage
    (Alaska, USA) 23
ash 9, 11, 12, 14, 30

Biscuit Plates activity 7

cinder cone volcanoes 9, 29
composite cone volcanoes
    9, 29
craters 8, 29

damage 20–23

Earthquake Challenge
    activity 20
earthquake drills 26, 27
earthquake-resistant
    buildings 20, 21
earthquakes 5, 7, 16–23, 24,
    26–27, 30, 31
earthquake waves 18
Earth's core 6, 29
Earth's crust 6, 16, 29
Earth's mantle 6, 16, 29
emergency kits 27, 29
eruption columns 11, 29
eruptions 4, 8, 10–13, 14
Eyjafjallajökull (Iceland)
    12, 31

faults 16–17, 18, 29
focus 18, 29

GPS movement sensor 15

Heat-resistant Materials
    activity 15

Kilauea (Hawaii) 13
Kobe (Japan) 23
Krakatoa (Indonesia) 13

lava 4, 10, 11, 13, 14, 29, 30
lava flows 10, 14, 29

magma 4, 8, 10, 15, 16, 29
magma chambers 8, 29
Model Seismograph
    activity 19
molten rock 4, 8, 9
Montserrat 31

Olympus Mons (Mars) 12

Popcorn Cinder Cone
    activity 9
Practice an Earthquake
    Drill activity 27

rescue dogs 26
rescue work 26–27
Ring of Fire 13, 31
rock 4, 6, 8, 9, 10

San Andreas Fault (USA)
    16, 31
San Francisco 22
Sandpit Volcano activity 11
seismographs 18, 19, 29
seismologists 18, 29
shield volcanoes 9, 29
Sinking Soil activity 23
Sliding Sandwiches
    activity 17

tectonic plates 6, 7, 16, 23,
    29, 31
Tsunami Tank activity 25
tsunamis 23, 24–25, 29, 31

underwater volcanoes 8

vents 8, 29
Volcano Map-maker
    activity 13
volcanoes 4, 7, 8–15, 30, 31
volcanologists 14, 15, 29